The Ancient Irish Goddess of War

By

W. M. Hennessey

First published in 1870

Published by Left of Brain Books

Copyright © 2023 Left of Brain Books

ISBN 978-1-397-66583-6

First Edition

All rights reserved. No part of this publication may be reproduced, distributed, or transmitted in any form or by any means, including photocopying, recording, or other electronic or mechanical methods, without the prior written permission of the publisher, except in the case of brief quotations permitted by copyright law. Left of Brain Books is a division of Left Of Brain Onboarding Pty Ltd.

PUBLISHER'S PREFACE

About the Book

"The Morrígan is usually interpreted as a "war goddess": W.M. Hennessey's "The Ancient Irish Goddess of War," written in 1870, was influential in establishing this interpretation.

The Morrígan ("terror" or "phantom queen") or Mórrígan ("great queen") (aka Morrígu, Morríghan, Mor-Ríoghain) is a figure from Irish mythology who appears to have once been a goddess, although she is not explicitly referred to as such in the texts.

She is usually seen as a terrifying figure. She is associated with war and death on the battlefield, sometime appearing in the form of a carrion crow, premonitions of doom, and with cattle. She is often considered a war deity comparable with the Germanic Valkyries, although her association with cattle also suggests a role connected with fertility and the land.

She is often interpreted as a triple goddess, although membership of the triad varies: the most common combination is the Morrígan, the Badb and Macha, but sometimes includes Nemain, Fea, Anann and others."

(Quote from wikipedia.org)

CONTENTS

PUBLISHER'S PREFACE
   THE ANCIENT IRISH GODDESS OF WAR 1
ENDNOTES 36

THE ANCIENT IRISH GODDESS OF WAR

THE discovery of a Gallo-Roman inscription, figured in the Revue Savoisienne of 15th November, 1867, and republished by M. Adolphe Pictet in the Revue Archéologique for July, 1868, forms the subject of one of those essays from the pen of the veteran philologist for which the students of Celtic languages and archæology cannot be sufficiently thankful. [1]

The inscription, the initial letter of which has been destroyed by an injury to the stone on which it is cut, reads: athuboduæ Aug[ustæ] Servilia Terenta [votum] s[olvit] l[ibens] m[erito].

M. Pictet's essay is entitled "Sur une Déese Gauloise de la Guerre"; and if he is right in his suggestion (which is very probably) that the letter destroyed was a c, and that ATHUBODVÆ should be read CATHUBODVÆ, the title is not inappropriate; and in the CATHUBODVÆ of the inscription we may recognise the badb-catha of Irish mythology.

The etymology of the name athubodua, or cathubodua, as we may venture to read it, has been examined with great industry by M. Pictet, who has managed to compress within the narrow limits of his essay a great mass of illustrative facts and evidences drawn from all the sources accessible to him. The first member of the name (cathu, = Irish cath, «pugna») presents but little difficulty to a Celtic scholar like M. Pictet, who would however prefer finding it written catu, without aspiration, as more nearly approaching the rigid orthography of Gaulish names, in which it is very frequently found as the first element; but the second member, bodua, although entering largely into the composition of names amongst all the nations of Celtic origin from the Danube to the islands of Aran, is confessedly capable of explanation only through the medium of the Irish, with its corresponding forms of bodb or badb (pron. bov or bav), originally signifying rage, fury, or violence and ultimately implying a witch, fairy, or goddess, represented by the bird known as the scare-crow, scald-crow, or Royston-crow, not the raven as M. Pictet seems to think.

The etymology of the name being examined, M. Pictet proceeds to illustrate the character of the Badb, and her position in Irish fairy mythology, by the help of a few brief and scarcely intelligible references from the printed books, the only materials accessible to him, but finds himself unable to complete his task, "for want of sufficient details," as he observes more than once.

The printed references, not one of which has escaped M. Pictet's industry are no doubt few, but the ancient tracts, romances, and battle pieces preserved in our Irish MSS. teem with details respecting this Badb-catha and her so-called sisters, Neman, Macha, and Morrigan or Morrigu (for the name is written in a double form), who are generally depicted as furies, witches, or sorceresses, able to confound whole armies, even in the assumed form of a bird.

Popular tradition also bears testimony to the former widespread belief in the magical powers of the Badb. In most parts of Ireland the Royston-crow, or fennóg liath na gragarnaith ("the chattering grey fennóg"). As she is called by the Irish speaking people, is regarded at the present day with feelings of mingled dislike and curiosity by the peasantry, who remember the many tales of depredation and slaughter in which the cunning bird is represented as exercising a sinister influence. Nor is this superstition confined to Ireland alone. The popular tales of Scotland and Wales, which are simply the echo of similar stories once current and still not quite extinct in Ireland, contain requent allusion to this mystic bird. The readers of the Mabinogion will call to mind, amongst other instances, the wonderful crows of Owain, prince of Rheged, a contemporary of Arthur, which always secured factory by the aid of the three hundred crows under its command [2]: and in Campbell's Popular Tales of the West Highlands we have a large stock of legends, in most of which the principal fairy agency is exercised by the hoodie or scare-crow.

It may be observed, by the way, that the name hoody, formerly applied by the Scotch to the hooded crow or the scare-crow, from its appearance, is now generally applied to its less intelligent relative the common carrion crow. But the hoody of Highland fairy mythology is, nevertheless, the same as the badb or Royston crow.

I have referred to Neman, Macha, and Morrigu, as the so called sisters of the Badb. Properly speaking, however, the name Badb seems to have been thee distinctive title of the mythological beings supposed to rule over battle and carnage. M. Pictet feels a difficulty in deciding whether there were three such beings, or whether Neman, Macha, and Morrigu are only three different names for the same goddess; but after a careful examination of the subject I am inclined to believe that these names represent three different characters, the attributes of Neman being like those of a being who confounded her victims with madness, whilst Morrigu incited to deeds of valour, or planned strife and battle, and Macha revelled amidst the bodies of the slain.

The popular notions regarding the identity of the battle furies with the royston-crow are accurately given in the Irish Dictionary compiled by the late Peter O'Connell, an excellent Irish scholar, who died some 60 years ago, and the original of whose excellent vocabulary is preserved in the British Museum. Thus:

Badb-catha is explained "finnóg, a royston crow, a squall crow".

"Badb, i.e. bean sidhe, a female fairy, phantom, or spectre, supposed to be attached to certain families, and to appear sometimes in the form of squall crows, or royston crows".

"Macha; i.e. a royston crow".

"Morrighain; i.e. the great fairy".

"Neamhan; i.e. Badb catha nó feannóg; a badb catha or a royston crow".

Similar explanations are also given by the other modern glossaries.

The task of elucidating the mythological character of these fairy queens has not been rendered easier by the labours of the etymologists, from Cormac to O'Davoren. Thus, in Cormac's glossary, Nemain is said to have been the wife of Neit, "the god of battle with the pagan Gaeidhel". In the Battle of Magh-Rath (O'Donovan's ed. p. 241) she is called Be nith gubhach Neid, "the battle-terriffic Be-Neid", or "wife of Neid". In an Irish MS. In Trin. Coll., Dublin class H, 3, 18, p.73 col. 1), Neit is explained "guin duine .i. gaisced; dia catha. Nemon a ben, u test Be Neid;". A poem in the Book of Leinster(fol. 6, a2), couples Badb and Neman as the wives of Neid or Neit:—

Neit mac Indui sa di mnai,
Badb ocus Nemaind cen goi,
Ro marbtha in Ailiuch cen ail,
La Neptuir d'Fhomorchaibh.

"Neit son of Indu, and his two wives,
Badb and Neamin, truly,
Were slain in Ailech, without blemish,
By Neptur of the Fomorians".

At folio 5, a2, of the same MS., Fea and Nemain are said to have been Neit's two wives; and if Fea represents Badb, we have a good notion of the idea entertained of her character, for Cormac states that Fea meant "everything most hateful".

But in the poem on Ailech printed from the Dinnsenchus in the "Ordinance Memoir of Templemore" (p. 226), Nemain only is mentioned as the wife of Neit, from whom Ailech was called Ailech-Neit; and it is added that she was brought from Bregia, or Meath.

In the Irish books of genealogy, Fea and Neman are said to have been the two daughters of Elcmar of the Brugh (Newgrange, near the Boyne), who was the son of Delbaeth, son of Ogma, son of Elatan, and the wives of Neid son of Indae, from whom Ailech-Neid is named.

Badb, Macha, and Morrigan (who is also called Ana, are described as the three daughters of Delbaeth son of Neid. And it is stated that Ernmas, daughter of Ettarlamh, son of Nuada Airged-lamh (King of the Tuatha-de-Danann), was the mother of the five ladies.

In other authorities, however Morrigan is said to have been Neit's wife. For instance, in the very ancient tale called Tochmarc Emhire, or Courtship of Emir, fragments of which are p[reserved in the Lebor na hUidhre and the book of Fermoy, Morrigan is described as "an badb catha, ocus is fria idberiur Bee Neid, i.e. bandea in cathae, uair is inan Neid ocus dia catha; "i.e. "the badb of battle; and of her is said Bee-Neid, i.e. goddess of battle, for Neid is the same as god of battle". A gloss in the Lebor Buidhe Lecain explains Machæ thus: "badb, no asi an tres Morrigan; mesrad machæ, .i. cendæ doine iar na nairlech;" i.e. "a scald crow; or she is the third Morrigan (great queen); Macha's fruit crop, i.e. the heads of men that have been slaughtered:. The same explanation, a little amplified, is also given in the MS. H. 3. 18. Trin Coll., Dublin(p. 82, col.2) where the name Badb is written Bodb, as it is elsewhere, and it is added that Bodb, Macha, and Morrigan were the three Morrigna. In the same glossary under the word be neit, we have the further explanation:—"Neit nomen viri; Nemhon a ben; ba neim-nech in lanomuin; be ben i.e. in badhb, ocus net cath, ocus olca diblinuib; inde dicitur beneit fort". i.e. "Neit nomen viri; Nehmon was his woman (wife); venomous were the pair; be a woman, i.e. the badhb, and net is battle; and both were evil; inde dicitur beneit fort ("evil upon thee"). Another gloss in the same collection, on the word gudomain, bears on the subject under consideration. It is as follows:—Gudomain, .i. fennoga no bansigaidhe; ut est glaidhomuin goa, .i. na demuin goach, na morrigna; no go conach demain iat na bansigaide go connach demain iffrin iat acht demain aeoir na fendoga; no eamnait andlaedha na sinnaigh, ocus eamnait a ngotha na fendoga;" i.e. "gudomain, i.e. scald crows or fairy women; utest glaidhumuin goahe false demons; it is false that the fendoga(scald crows) are not hellish but aery demons: the foxes double their cries, but the fennoga double their sounds". To understand this curious gloss it is necessary to add that in a previous one the word glaidomuin is explained as signifying sinnaig, or maic tire (foxes or wolves), because in barking they double their sound; glaidomuin being understood by the glossarist as glaid-emain, i.e. "double call", from glaid, "call", and enain "double," while the crow only doubles the sound, gath-emain, "double-sound". Cormac explains guidemainas uatha ocus morrigna, i.e. "spectres and great queens".

Let us take leave of these etymological quibbles, and examine the mythological character of the badb, as portrayed in the materials still remaining to us.

As mostly all the supernatural beings alluded to in Irish fairy lore are referred to the Tuatha-de-Danann. The older copies of the Lebor Gabhala, or "Book of Occupation" that preserved in the Book of Leinster for instance, specifies Badb, Macha, and Ana (from the latter of whom are named the mountains called da cich Anann, or the Paps, in Kerry), as the daughters of Ernmas, one of the chiefs of that mythical colony. Badb ocus Macha ocus Anand, diatat cichi Anand il- Luachair, tri ingena Ernbais, na ban tuathige; "Badb, and Macha, and Anand from whom the "paps of Anann [3]" in Luachair are [called], the three daughters of Ernmais, the ban-tuathaig". In an accompanying versification of the same statement the name of Anand or Ana, however, is changed to Morrigan:—

"Badb is Macha mét indbáis,
Morrigan fotla felbáis,
Indlema ind ága ernbais,
Ingena ana Ernmais [4]

"Badb and Macha, rich in store,
Morrigan who dispenses confusion,
Compassers of death by the sword,
Noble daughters of Ernmas".

It is important to observe that Morrigan is here identified with Anann, or Ana (for Anann is the gen. form); and in Cormac's Glossary Ana is described as "Mater deorum Hibernensium; robu maithdin rosbiathadsi na dee de cujus nominee da cich Nanainne iar Luachair nominantur ut fertur;" i.e. "Mater deorum Hibernensium; well she used to nourish the gods de cujus nominee the 'two paps of Ana' in west Luachair are named" Under the name Buanand the statement is more briefly repeated. The historian Keating enumerates Badb, Macha, and Morrighan as the three goddesses of the Tuatha-de-Danann; but he is silent as to their attributes. It would seem, however, that he understood Badb to be the proper name of one fairy, and not a title for the great fairy queens.

In the Irish tales of war and battle, the Badb is always represented as foreshadowing, by its cries, the extent of the carnage about to take place, or the death of some eminent personage. Thus in the ancient battle-story, called Bruiden da Choga, the impending death of Cormac Condloinges, the son of Conor Mac Nessa, is foretold in these words:—

"Badb bel derg giarfid fon tech;
Bo collain bet co sirtech."

"The red-mouthed Badbs will cry around the house,
For bodies they will be solicitious."

And again—

"Grecfaidit badba banae"
"Pale badbs shall shriek."

In the very ancient tale called Tochmarc Feirbe, or the "Court-ship of Ferb:, a large fragment of which is rpeserved in the Book of Leinster, the druid Ollgaeth, prophesying the death of Mani, the son of Queen Medb, through the treachery of King Conor Mac Nessa, says:—

"Brisfid badb
Bid brig borb,
　Tolg for Medb;
Ilar écht,
Ar for slùag,
　Trúag in deilm [5].

"Badb will break;
Fierce power will be
　Hurled at Medbh;
Many deeds—
Slaughter upon the host—

Alas! the uproar."

In the account of the battle of Cnucha (or Castleknock, near Dublin), preserved in a 14th century MS., the druid Cunallis, foretelling the slaughter, says:—"Biagh bádba os bruinnibh na bfear" "Badbs will be over the breasts of men [6]."

In the description of the battle of Magh-Tuiredh, it is said that just as the great conflict was about to begin, the "badbs, and bledlochtana, and idiots shouted so that the were heard in clefts and in cascades, and in the cavitites of the earth;" "badba ocus bledlocktana, ocus amaite, go clos anallaib, ocus a nesaib, ocus a fothollaib in talnian [7]."

In the battle of Magh-Rath it is the "gray-haired Morrigu "(scald-crow), that shouts victory over the head of Domhnall son of Ainmire, as Dubgdiadh sings (O'Donovan's ed. p. 198):—

"Fuil os a chind ag eigmigh
Caillech lom, luath ag leimnig
Os eannaib a narm sa sciath,
Is i in Morrigu mongliath."

"Over his head is shrieking
A lean hag, quickly hopping
Over the points of their weapons and shields—
She is the gray-haired Morrigu."

In the account of the massacre of the Irish Kings by the Aithech-tuatha, preserved in the Book of Fermoy, it is stated that after the nmassacre "ba forbhailidh badhbh derg dasachta, ocus ba bronach banchuire don treis sin;" "Gory Badb was joyful, and women were sorrowful, for that conflict."

In the enumeration of the birds and demons that assembled to gloat over the slaughter about to ensue from the clash of the combatants at the battle of Glontarf, the badb is assigned the first place. The description is truly terrible, and affords a painful picture of the popular superstition at the time. "Ro erig em badb discir, dian, demnetach, dasachtach, dúr, duabsech, detcengtach, cruaid, croda, cosaitech, co bai ic screchád ar luamain, os a cennaib. Ro eirgetar am bananaig, ocus boccanaig, ocus geliti glinni, ocus amati adgaill, ocus siabra, ocus seneoin, ocus damna admilti aeoir ocus firmaminti, ocus siabarsluag debil demnach, co mbatar a comgresacht ocus i commorad aig ocus irgaili leo."

"There arose a wild, impetuous, precitpitate, mad, inexorable, furious, dark, lacerating, merciless, combative, contentious badb, which was shrieking and fluttering over their heads. And there arose also the satyrs, and sprites, and the maniacs of the valleys, and the witches, and goblins, and owls, and destroying demons of the air and firmament, and the demoniac phantom host; and they were inciting and sustaining valour and battle with them."—"Cogadh Gaedhel re Gallaibh," Todd's ed., p. 174.

So also in the account of the battle fought between the men of Leinster and Ossory, in the year 870, contained in the Brussels "Fragments of Irish Annals," the appearance of the badb is followed by a great massacre: "As mór tra an toirm ocus an fothrom baoi eturra an uair sin, ocus ra togaibh badbh cenn eturra, ocus baoi marbhadh mór eturra san cán;" i.e. "great indeed was the din and tumult that prevailed between them at this time, and Badb appeared among them, and there was great destruction between them to and fro."

But the Badbs could to more than scream and flutter. Thus we read in the first battle of Magh-Tuiredh, that when the Tuatha-de-Danann had removed to the fastness of Connacht, to Sliabh-Belgadain, or Cenn-duibh-slebhe, that Badb, Macha, and Morrigu exercised their magical powers to keep the Fir-bolgs in ignorance of the westward movement. The text is from H. 2. 17. T. C. D., fol. 93, col 2. "Is annsin do chuaidh Badhbh ocus Macha ocus Morrighu gu cnoc gabala na ngial, ocus gu tulaig techtairechta na trom sluag, gu Temraig, ocus do feradar cetha dolfe draigechta, ocus cith nela cotaigecha ciath, ocus frasa tromaidble tened, ocus dortad donnfala do shiltin asin aeor i cennaib ne curad, ocus nir legset scarad na scailed do feraib Bold co cenn tri la ocus tri naidche." "Then the Badb, and Macha, and Morrigu went to the hill of hostage-taking, the tulach which heavy hosts frequented, to Temhair (Tara), and they shed druidically formed showers, and fog-sustaining shower-clouds, and poured down from the air, about the heads of the warriors, enormous masses of fire, and streams of red blood; and they did not permit the Fir-Bolgs to scatter or separate for the space of three days and three nights." It is stated, however, that the Fir-Bolg druids ultimately overcame this sorcery. And in the battle of Magh-Tuiredh they are represented as assisting the Tuatha-de-Danann. Thus, in the account of the third day's conflict we read.—"Is iad taisig ro ergedar re Tuathaib de Danann isin lo sin .i. Ogma ocus Midir ocus Bodb derg ocus Diancecht, ocus Aengaba na hiruaithe. Rachmaitne lib ar na ingena .i. Badb ocus Macha, ocus Morrigan, ocus Danann;" i.e. "The chieftains who assisted the Tuatha-de-Danannon that day were Ogma, and Midir, and Bodb Derg, and Diancecht, and Aebgabha of Norway. 'We will go with you,' said the daughters, viz:—Badb, andMacha, and Morrigan, and Danann (or Anann)." H. 2. 17, fol. 95, col. 2.

Another instance of the warlike prowess of these fairies is related in a curious mythological tract preserved in the Books of Lismore and Fermoy. I refer to the Hallow-eve dialogue between the fairy Rothniab and Finghen Mach-Luchta, in which the fairy enumerates the several mystical virtues attached to that pagan festival, and amongst others the following, referring to an incident arising from the battle of the Northern Magh-Tuiredh, or "Magh-Tuiredh of the Fomorians." "Ocus cidh buadh aile, for Fingen. Ni ansam, for in ben. Ata ann cethrar atrullaiset ria Tuathaib de Danann a cath Muigi tuired, corrabatar oc coll etha ocus blechta, ocus messa, ocus murthorad .i. fer dib a slemnaib Maigi Itha .i. Redg a ainmsidé; fer dib a sléib Smóil .i. Grenu a ainmsidé;fer aile a ndromannaib Breg .i. Bréa a ainm; fer aile dib hi crichaib cruachna .i. Tinel a ainmsidé. Indocht rosruithéa a hErinn .i. in Morrigan ocus Badb Side Femin, ocus Midir Brig Leith, ocus Mac ind óc, conna beth foglai Fomóir for hErinn cu brath."

"'And what other virtue, 'asked Finghen. 'Not difficult to tell," said the woman. There were four persons who fled before the Tuatha-de-Danann from the battle of Magh-Tuiredh, so that they were ruining corn, and milk, and fruit-crops, and sea produce; viz: one of them in Slemna-Maighe-Itha, whose mane was Redg; one of them in SliabhSmoil, whose mane was Grenu; another man of them in Dromanna-Cruachan, whose mane was Tinel. This night [i.e. on a similar night] they were expelled from Eriu by the Morrigan, and by Badb of sidh-Femain,and by Midir of Brig-leith, and Mac-ind-oig, so that Fomorian depredators should never more be over Eriu." Book of Fermoy, 24, b2.

In the grand old Irish epic of the Tain Bo Cuailnge, Badb (or Bodb) plays a very important part. Neman confounds armies, so that friendly bands fall in mutual slaughter whilst Macha is pictured as a fury that riots and revels among the slain. But certainly the grandest figure is that of Morrigu, whose presence intensifies the hero, nerves his arm for the cast, and guides the course of the unerring lance. As in this epic the first place in valour and prowess is given to Cuchullain, the Hector of the

Gaeidhel, it is natural to expect that he should be represented as the special favourite of the supernatural powers. And so it is; for we read that the Tuatha-de-Danann endowed him with great attributes. In that passage of the Tain where Cuchullain is described as jumping into his chariot to proceed to fight Firdia Mac Demain, the narrative says (Book of Leinster, fol. 57, b2) "ra gairestar imme boccanaig, ocus banánaig, ocus geniti glinni, ocus demna aeoir, daig dabertis Tuatha de Danann a ngasciud immisium, combad móti a grain, ocus a ecla, ocus a urúaman in cach cath ocus in cach cathrói, in cach comlund ocus in cach comruc i teiged;" "the satyrs, and sprites, and maniacs of the valleys, and demons of the air shouted about him, for the Tuatha-de-Danann were wont to impart their valour to him, in order that he might be more feared, more dreaded, more terrible, in every battle and battle-field, in every combat and conflict, into which he went." So, when the forces of Queen Medb arrive at Magh-Tregham, in the present county of Longford, on the way to Cuailnge, Neman appears amongst them. "Dosfobair tra ind Nemain .i. in Badb lasodain, ocus nipsísin adaig bá samam doib la budris ocus focherd dirna mor dint slógh conluid Medbh dia chosc" "Then the Neman, i.e. Badb, attacked them, and that was not the most comfortable night with them, from the uproar of the giant Dubtach through his sleep. The bands were immediately startled, and the army confounded, until Medb went to check the confusion." Lebor na hUidhre, fol. 46, b1.

And in another passage, in the episode called "Breslech Maighe Muirthemhne," where a terrible description is given of Cuchullain's fury at seeing the hostile armies of the south and west encamped within the borders of Uladh, we are told (Book of Leinster, fol.54, a2, and b1):

"Atchonnairc seom uad gristaitnem na narm nglan orda os chind chethri noll choiced nErend refuiniud nell na nona. Do fainig ferg ocus luinni mor icanaiscin re ilar a bidbad, re immad a namad, Rogab a da shleig, ocus a sciath, ocus a chlaideb, Crothais a sciath, ocus cressaigis a shlega, ocus bertnaigis a chlaidem, ocus do bert rem curad as a bragit cororecratar bananaig ocus boccanaig, ocus geniti glinni, ocus demna aeoir, re uathgrain nag are dosbertatar ar aird, co ro mesc ind Neamain .i. in Badb forsint slog. Dollotar in armgrith cethri choiced hErend im rennaib a sleg ocus a narm fadessin, conerbaltatar ced laech dib d'uathbas ocus chridemnas ar lar in dunaid ocus in longphoirt in naidchisin." "He saw from him the ardent sparkling of the bright golden weapons over the heads of the four great provinces of Eriu, before the fall of the cloud of evening. Great fury and indignation seized him on seeing them, at the number of his opponents and at the multitude of his enemies. He seized his two spears, and his shield and his sword, and uttered from his throat a warrior's shout, so that sprites, and satyrs, and maniacs of the valley, and the demons of the air responded, terror-stricken by the shout which he had raised on high. And the Neman, i.e. the Badb, confused the army; and the four provinces of Eriu dashed themselves against the points of their own spears and weapons, so that one hundred warriors died of fear and trembling in the middle of the fort and encampment that night."

Of the effects of this fear inspired by the Badb was geltacht or lunacy, which, according to the popular notion, affected the body no less than the mind, and, in fact, made its victims so light that they flew through the air like birds. A curious illustration of this idea is afforded by the history of Suibhne, son of Colman Cuar, king of Dal-Araidhe, who became panic-stricken at the battle of Magh-Rath, and performed extraordinary feats of agility. Another remarkable instance will be found in the Fenian Romance called Cath-Finntragha (Battle of Ventry Harbour), where Bolcan, a king of France, is stated to have been seized with geltacht at the sight of Oscur, son of Oisin, so that he jumped into the air, alighting in the beautiful valley called Glenn-na-ngealt (or "the Glen of the Lunatics"), twenty miles to the east of Ventry Harbour, whither, in the opinion of the past generation, all the lunatics of the country would go, if unrestrained, to feed on the cure-imparting water cresses that grow there over the well called Tobar na ngealt, or the "well of the lunatics". In the same tale it is also said that those who heard the shouts of the invading armies on landing were surprised that they were not carried away by the wind and lunacy: "ba hiongna le gach dá gcúaladna garrtha sin gan dol re gaoith agus re gealtachus doib." Persons are also represented as frightened to madness on observing the fight between Cuchullain and Ferdia, which forms the chief episode in the Tain bo Cuailgne.

Again, in the battle of Almha (or the Hill of Allen, near Kildare), fought in the eyar 722, between Murchadh, king of Laighen, and Ferghal, monarch of Ireland, where "the red- mouthed, sharp-beaked badb croaked over the head of Ferghal," ("ro lao badb belderg biorach iolach um cenn Fergaile"), we are told that nine persons became thus affected. The Four Masters (A.D. 718) represent them as "fleeing in panic and lunacy," (do lotar hi faindeal ocus I ngealtacht). Other annalists describe them in similar terms. Thus, Mageoghegan, in his translation of the "Annals of Clonmacnoise," says they "flyed in the air as if they were winged fowle." O'Donovan (in notes to the entries in his edition of the Four Masters, and Fragments of Annals) charges Mageoghegan with misrepresenting the popular idea; but Mageoghegan represented it correctly, for in the Chronicum Scotorum the panic-stricken at this battle are called "volatiles," or gealta. May we not therefore seek, in this vulgar notion, the origin of the word "flighty" as applied to persons of eccentric mind?

But although, as we have seen, the assistance given to Cuchullain by Neman was both frequent and important, the intervention of Morrigu in his behalf is more constant. Nay, he seems to have been the object of her special care. She is represented as meeting him sometimes in the form of a woman, but frequently in the shape of a bird—most probably a crow. Although, apparently, his tutelary goddess, the Morrigu seems to have been made the instrument, through the decree of a cruel fate, in his premature death. The way was thus:

In the territory of Cuailnge, near the Fews Mountains, dwelt a famous bull, called the Donn Cuailgne (or Brown [Bull] of Cuailgne), a beast so huge that thrice fifty youths disported themselves on his back together. A certain fairy, living in the caves of Cruachan, in the county of Roscommon, had a cow, which she bestowed on her mortal husband, Nera, and which the Morrigu carried off to the great Donn Cualgne, and the calf that issued from this association was fated to be the cause of the Tain Bo Cuailgne. The event is told in the tale called Tain Be Aingen, one of the prefatory stories to the great epic, which thus speaks of the Morrigan. "Berid in Morrigan iarum boin a mic sium cen bai seom ina cotlad, conderodart in Donn Cuailgne tair i Cuailgne. Do thaet cona boin doridise anair, Nostaertend Cuchullain i Mag Murthemne oc tuidecht tairis, ar ba do gesaib Conculaind ce teit ban as a thir manib udairc les. . . . . . Da thairte Cuchullain in Morrigan, cona boid, ocus isbert ni berthar in nimirce, ol Cuchullain," i.e. "The Morrigan afterwards carried off his [Nera's] son's cow, so that the Donn Cuailgne consorted with her in the east in Cuailgne. She went westward again with the cow. Cuchullain met with her in Magh-Muirthemhne whilst crossing over it; for it was of Cuchullain's prohibitions that even a woman should leave his territory unless he wished. . . . . . Cuchullain overtook the Morrigan, and he said: the cow shall not be carried off." But the Morrigan whom Cuchullain probably did not recognise in the form of a woman, succeeds in restoring the cow to her owner.

All the while, Morrigan seems to watch over the interests of the Ultonians. Thus when, after the death of Lethan at the hands of Cuchullain, Medbh endeavoured, by a rapid and bold movement, to surround and take possession of the Donn Cuailgne, we find her acquainting the Donn Cuailgne with the danger of his position, and advising him to retire into the impenetrable fastness of the Fews.

"Is he in la cetna tanic in Dond Cuailgne co crich margin, ocus coica samseisce immi do samascib. . . . . is e in la cetna tanic in Morrigu, ingen Ernmais a sibaib [in deilb euin] comboi for in chorthi i Temair Chualgne ic brith rabuid don Dund Chualgne ria ferdaib hErend, ocus rogab ac a acallaim; ocus maith, a thruaig, a duind Cuailnge ar in Morrigu, deni fatchius daig ardotreset fir hErenn, ocus not berat dochum longphoirt mani dena faitchius; ocus ro gab ic breith rabuid do samlaid, ocus dosbert na briathrasa ar aird."

"It was on that very day that the Donn Cuailgne came to Crich-Margin, and fifty heifers of the heifers about him. . . . . . It was the same day Morrigu, daughter of Ernmas, from the Sidhe, came [in the form of a bird—Lebor na hUidhre] and perched on the pillar stone in Temair of Cuailnge, giving notice to the Donn Cuailnge before the men of Erui; and she proceeded to speak with him, and said, 'Well thou poor thing, thou Donn Cuailnge; take care, for the men of Eriu will come to thee, and they will take thee to their fortress if you do not take care. 'And she went on warning him in this wise, and uttered these words aloud." . . . . . [Here follows a short and very obscure poem to the same effect], Book of Leinster, fol. 50, a1.

Immediately after the foregoing incident the narrative, as preserved in the Lebor na hUidhre, represents Cuchullain and Morrigu as playing at cross-purposes. I have suggested that Cuchullain did not appear to recognise the Morrigu when she met him in the form of a woman, in the scene quoted from the Tain Be Aingen. He seems similarly ignorant of her identity on other occasions, when she is said to have presented herself before him in female shape. Let us take, for example, the episode entitled "Imacallaim na Morigna fri Coincullain,"—"Dialogue of the Morrigan with Cuchullain, "which preceeds his fight with Loch, son of Ernonis.

"Conacca Cu in nocben chuci conetuch cacn datha impe, ocus delb ro derscaigthe fuirri. Ce taisiu or Cu. Ingen Buain ind rig, or si; do deochaidh cuchutsa; rotcharus ar thairscelaib, ocus tucuc mo seotu lim, ocus mo indili. Ni maith, em, ind inbuid tonnanac, nach is olc ar mblath oinmgorti. Ni haurusa damsa dana comrac fri banscail cein nombeo isind nith so. Bid im chobairse daitsiu (.i. do gensa congnom latt) oc sudiu. Ni ar thoin mna dana gabussa inso. Bi ansu daitsiu, or si, in tan doragsa ar do chend oc comrac fris na firu; doragsa irricht escongan for chossaib issind ath co taithis. Dochu lim, on, oldas ingen rig; notgebsa, or se, im ladair commebsat t'asnai, ocus bia fond anim sin co ro secha brath bennachtan fort. Timorcsa in cethri forsind ath do dochumsa irricht soide glaisse. Leicfesa cloich daitsiu as in tailm co commart do suil it cind, ocus bia fond anim co ro secha brath bennachtan fort. To rach dait irricht samaisci maile derce riasind eit, comensat forsnai lathu, ocus fors na hathu, ocus fors na liniu, ocus nimaircechasa ar do chend. Tolecubsa cloich deitsiu or se, commema do fergara fot, ocus bia fo ind anim sin co ro secha brath bennachtan fort. Lasodain teit uad."

"Cu saw the young woman dressed in garments of every hue, and of most distinguished form, approaching him. 'Who art thou?' asked Cu. 'The daughter of Buan, the King,' said she; 'I have come to thee; I have loved thee for they renown, and have brought with me my jewels and my cattle.' 'Not good is the time thou hast come,' said he,' said he. 'It is not easy for me to associate with a woman whilst I may be engaged in this conflict.' 'I will be of assistance to thee therein,' replied she. 'Not by woman's favour have I come here, 'responded Cuchullain. "Twill be hard for thee,' said she, 'when I go against thee whilst encountering men. I will go in the form of an eel under thy feet, in the ford, so that thou shalt fall.' 'More likely, indeed, than a king's daughter; but I will grasp thee between my fingers,' said he 'so that thy ribs shall break, and thou shalt endure that blemish forever.' 'I will collect the cattle upon the ford towards thee, in the shape of a grey-hound,' said she, 'I shall hurl a stone at thee from the sling,' said he, 'which will break thine eye in the head; and thou shalt be under that blemish for ever.' 'I will go against thee in the form of a red hornless heifer before the herd, and they shall defile the pools, and fords, and linns, and thou shalt not find me there before thee' 'I will fling a stone at thee,' said he 'which will break thy right leg under thee; and thou shalt be under that blemish for ever,' With that she departed from him."

In some MSS. The foregoing dialogue forms the principal feature in a romantic tale called Tain Bo Rgeamhna, which, like the Tain Be Aingen, is one of the prefatory stories to the great Cattle Spoil. Like the Tain Be Aingen, also, it introduces the Morrigu in the character of a messenger of the fate that had decreed the death of Cuchullain when the issue of the Donn Cuailnge and the Connacht cow should have attained a certain age. But the Tain Bo Regamhna is further important, as connecting the Morrigu with Cuchullain, in the position of protector. The tale, which is too long to quote in extenso, represents Cuchullain as one morning meeting the Morrigu in the form of a red-haired woman, driving a cow through the plain of Murthemne, as related in Tain Be Aingen. Cuchullain, in his quality of guardian of the border district, tries to prevent her from proceeding; and after a great deal of argument during which Cuchullain seems not to know his opponent, the woman and cow disappear, and Cuchullain percieves that she has become transformed into a bird, which perches on an adjacent tree. Cuchullain, as soon as he become aware that he had been contending with a supernatural being, confident in his own might, boasts that if he had known the character of his opponent, they would not have separated as they did; whereupon the following exchange of sentiments takes place:—

"Cid andarignisiu, ol si, rodbia olc de. Ni cuma dam ol Cuchullain. Cumcim eicin ol in ben; is ac [do] diten do baissiu, atusa ocus biad, olsi. Do fucus in mboinsea a sith Cruachan, condarodart in Dub Cuailnge lim i Cuailnge .i. tarb Dairi mic Fiachna, Ised aired biasu imbeathaid corop dartaig in laegh fil imbroind na bo so, ocus ise consaithbe Tain Bo Cuailnge. Bid am ardercusia de din tain ishin, ol Cuchullain. Gegna a nanrada, brisfe a mor chatha, bid a tigba na tana."

"'What hast thou done?' asked she; 'evil will ensue to thee therefrom,' 'I care not,' said Cuchullain. 'But I do,' said the woman (i.e. the bird or badb); it is protecting thee I was, am, and will be,' said she. 'I brought this cow from Sidh-Cruachna, so that the Dubh Cuailnge, i.e. Daire Mac Fiachna's bull, met her in Cuiailnge. The length of time you have to live is until the calf that is in this cow's body will be a yearling; and it is it that shall lead thee to the Tain bo Cuailnge.' 'I will be illustrious on account of that Tain,' observed Cuchullain; 'I shall wound their warriors break their great battles, and I will be in pursuit of the Tain.' (Lebor Buidhe Lecain col.648). Then the Morrigu threatens to act to Cuchullain in the way detailed in the dialogue which I have just quoted; and, as the tale concludes, "the Badb afterwards goes away." ("luid ass in Badb iarum").

The Morrigu puts her threats into execution during Cuchullain's fight with Loch, son of Ernonis. The narrative in Lebor na hUidhre describes the encounter in the following manner:—

" O ro chomraicset iarom ind fir for sind áth, ocus o rogabsat oc gliaid ocus oc imesorcain and, ocus o ro gab cach dib for truastad a chéli, focheird in escongon triol (.i. tri curu) im chossa Conculaind combói fáen fotarsnu isind áth ina ligu. Dauautat (.i. buailis) Loch cosin chlaidiub combu chroderg int ath dia fuilriud. . . . Lasodain atraig, ocus benaid in nescongain comebdatar a hasnai indi, ocus comboing in cethri dars na slúaga sair ar ecin, combertatar a puple innan adarcaib lasa torandcless darigensat in dá lathgáile isind ath. Tanautat som ind sod mactire do imairg na bú fair siar. Léicid som cloich as a tailm co mebaid a suil ina cind. Téite irricht samaisce máile derge, muitte rias na buaib forsna linni ocus na háthu. Is and asbert som ni airciu (.i. ni rochim) anáthu la linni. Leicidsom cloich dont samaisc máil déirg comemaid a ger gara foi." Lebor na hUidre, fol. 37, a1.

"When the men met afterwards in the ford, and when they commenced fighting, and assaulting, and when each man began to strike the other, the escongon (eel) made a triple twist round Cuchullain's legs, so that he was lying down prostrate across in the ford. Loch struck him with his sword, and the ford was gory-red from his blood. . . . . Thereupon he arose and struck the eel, so that her ribs broke in her. And the cattle rushed violently past the army, eastwards, carrying the tents on their horns, at the sound made by the two warriors in the ford. He (Cuchullain) drove to the west the wolf-hound that collected the cows against him; and cast a stone out of his sling at it, which broke its eye in its head. Then she (Morrigu) went in the shape of a short hornless red heifer before the cows, and advanced into the linns and fords; when he said—'I see not the fords with the pools.' He cast a stone at the red hornless heifer, and broke her leg." it is added that "it was then truly that Cuchullain did to the Morrigu the three things which he had promised to accomplish, in the Tain Bo Regamna;" (is andsin tra do géni Cuchullainn frisin Morrigain a tréde do rairngert di hi tain bó Regamna;" ib).

With respect to the instances of transformation already referred to it may be pertinent to quote the following, which is given in an account of the battle alleged to have been fought at Tailte between the Milesian forces and Eire, queen of Mac Greine, king of the Tuath-de-Danann, who acted in the capacity of a war goddess. The Milesian chiefs are represented as having advanced as far north as the hill of Uisnech, when it is added "go facadar in en mnai minderg moir malach dhuibh in deil bdesi . . . . da ninsaigidh. Ingantaigsed na sluaigh re sirdechsain ahinnell ocus a habaise. In darna huair ann ba rigan roisclethan ro alainn; ocus in uair aill . . . . na baidb biraigh banghlais. . . . . . Suidhis ar inchaib Eremoin; snaidmis a heinech ar Emir. Ca crich as ar cemnigis ocus ca cele ca clechtaidh do comluigi, ocus ca hainm is raiti rit a ingín, ar Eremon. O tuathaib digraisi de Denann do dechladhus am, bar, isi, 7 mac gréni gaiscedhach mfher cele, 7 Eriu mainmse, bar in ingen." "They saw the one woman, smooth-red, large, black-browed, in the shape of two . . . . . approaching them. The hosts wondered with constant observation of her behaviour and changefulness. At one moment she was a broad-eyed, most beautiful queen, and another time . . . . a beaked, white-grey badb. . . . . She sits down in the presence of Eremon; she enjoins her protection on Emir. 'What country hast thou come from, and what companion dost thou associate with, and what name is to be addressed to thee, o woman, asked Eremon. 'From the ardent Tuatha de Danann I have come truly,' said she, 'and Mac Greni, warrior, is my husband, and Eriu is my name, 'said the woman." Ms. H. 4. 22. p. 120.

And Aimhirgin asks, immediately after the preceding dialogue, "ca ni chuingi etir, a ingin ilrechtach;" what do you request, o woman of many shapes," the latter epithet being used in allusion to the frequent transformations referred to before. The account further represents her as fighting a battle with the chiefs in question, in the form of a badb.

The next meeting between Cuchullain and the Morrigan is very curious. It is thus related in the Book of Leinster fol. 54,a2.

"Andsin tanic in Mórrigu ingen Ernmais a sidaib irricht sentainne, corrabi ic blegu bó trí sine na fiadnaisse. Is immi tainic si sin ar bith a forithen do Choinchullaind; daid ni gonad Cuchullain nech ara térnád combeth cuit dó fein na legus. Conattech Cuchullain blegon fuirri iar na dechrad dittaid. Do brethasi blegon sini dó . Rop slán a neim damsa so. Ba slána lethrosc na rigna. Conaittecht som in tres ndig, ocus dobrethasi blegon sine dó. Bendacht dée ocus ándee fort a ingen (batar é a ndee int aes cumachta, ocus andee int aes trebaire); ocus ba slan ind rigan."

"then the Morrigu, daughter of Ernmas, came from the Sidhe, in the form of an old woman, and was milking a three-teated cow in his presence. The reason she came was, in order to be helped by Cuchullainn; for no one whom Cuchullainn wounded could recover unless he himself had some hand in the cure. Cuchullain asked her for milk, after having been troubled with thirst. She gave him the milk of one teat. "May I be safe from poison therefor." The queen's eye was cured. He asked her again for the milk of a teat. She gave it to him. "May the giver be safe from poison." He asked for the third drink, and she gave him the milk of a teat. "The blessings of gods and men be on thee, woman (the people of power were their gods, and the wise people were their andée "non divine:); and the queen was cured."

When the time approached in which Cuchullainn should succumb to the decree of fate, as previously announced to him by Morrigan, the impending loss of her favourite hero appears to have affected her with sorrow. The night before the fatal day when his head and spoils were borne off in triumph by Erc Mac Cairpre, Morrigan, we are told, disarranged his chariot, do delay his departure for the fated meeting.

Thus we read in the "Aided Conchullainn," or "Tragedy of Cuchullainn," contained in the Book of Leinster (fol. 77, a1) that when he approached his horse, the Liath Macha, in the last morning of his existence, this faithful companion of his many victories "thrice turned his left side" towards his master, as an augury of his doom so soon to await him; and he found that "the Morrigan had broken the chariot the night previous, for she liked not that Cuchullainn should go to the battle, as she knew that he would not again reach Emain Macha."

"Teite Cuchullainn adochum [in Leith Macha], ocus ro impa int ech a chle friss fothri, ocus roscail in Morrigu in carpat issind aidchi remi, ar nir bo ail le a dul Conculainn dochum in chatha, ar rofitir noco ricfad Emain Macha afrithis,"

Then follows a curious scene between Cuchullainn and Liath Macha or "grey horse of Macha," the hero reminding his steed of the time when the Badb accompanied them in their martial feats at Emain Macha, or Emania (rodonbai badb in Emain Macha), and the Liath, becoming so affected at the impending fate of his master, "co tarlaic a bolgdera móra fola for a dib traigthib," "that he dropped his big tears of blood on his (Cuchullain's) two feet."

The grief of the Liath Macha, and the arts of the Morrigu, were of no avail, Cuchullain would go to the field of battle, impelled by the unseen power which ruled his destiny. But before he approaches the foe, he meets with three female idiots, blind of the left eye, cooking a charmed dog on spits made of the rowan tree; creatures of hateful aspect and wicked purpose.

Cuchullain's strength must be annihilated, or the fates will have decreed in vain; and this can only be done through his partaking of the horrid dish, which he resolves to do rather than tarnish his chivalrous reputation by refusing the request of the witches, although aware of the tragic results about to ensue, The strength of the hero is paralyzed by the contact with the unclean food handed to him from the witch's left hand; and Cuchullainn rushes headlong to his doom. But still the Morrigan does not abandon him, although apparently quite powerless to assist him; for as he comes near to the enemy, "a bird of valour" is seen flying about over the chief in his chariot (en blaith, i.e. lon gaile, etarluamnach uasa erra oen charpait). And after he has received his death-wound she perches beside him awhile, before winging her flight to the fairy palace beside the Suir, from which she came. The following is the description of Cuchullainn's proceedings after receiving his mortal wound, extracted from the Book of Leinster (fol. 78, a2).

"Do dechuid iarum crich mór ond loch (Loch Lamraith in Magh Muirthemne) slar, ocus rucad a rosc airi, ocus téit dochum coirthi cloiche file isin maig cotarat a choimchriss immi, narablad na suidiu, nach ina ligu, conbad ina sessam atbalad. Is iarsin do echatar na fir immacuairt, ocus ni rolamsatar dul a dochum. Andarleo ropo beo. Is mebol duib, ol Erc Mac Cairpre, cen cend ind fhir do thabhairt lib in digail chind m'atarsa rucad leis co ro adnacht fri airsce Echdach Niafer. Rucad a chend assaide co fil i síd Nenta iar nusciu. . . . . Iarsin tra do dechaid in Liath Macha co Coinculaind dia imchoimét in céin robói a anim and, ocus ro mair in lon laith ass a étan. Is iarum bert in Liath Macha na tri derg ruathar immi ma cuairt, co torchair l. leis cona fiaclaib, ocus xxx cach crui do issed romarb dont sluag. Conid de ata nitathe buadremmend ind leith Macha iar marbad Conculainn. Conid iarsin dolliud ind ennach for a gualaind. Nir bo gnáth in corthe ut fo enaib ar Erc mac Carpre."

"He (Cuchullainn) then went westwards, a good distance from the lake (lock Lamraith in Magh Muirthemne), and looked back at it. And he went to a pillar stone which is in the plain, and placed his side against it, that he might not die sitting or lying, but that he might die standing. After this the men went all about him, but dared not approach him, for they thought he was alive. 'It is a shame for you,' said Erc Mac Cairpre, 'not to bring that man's head in retaliation for my father's head, which was borne off by him, and buried against Airsce Echdach Niafer. His head was taken from thence, so that it is in Sidh-Nenta. . . . . Afterwards, moreover, the Liath Macha went to Cuchullain, to guard him whilst his spirit lived in him, and whilst the lon laith (bird of valour?) continued out of his forehead. Then the Liath Macha executed the three red routs about him, when fifty men fell by his teeth, and thirty by each shoe, all of the enemy's host; and hence the proverb—'Not more furious was the victorious rout of the Liath Macha, after the killing of Cuchullain,'—Thereupon the bird went and perched near his shoulder. "That pillar stone was not usually the resort of birds," said Erc Mac Cairbre, who supposed the Morrigan to be a mere carrion crow awaiting the feast prepared by his hand. Then they advance and cut off Cuchullain's head, and the Morrigan disappears from the scene.

The exact meaning of the expressions en blaith, and lon gaile (called also lón or lúan-laith) which occur in the preceding sentences have not been well defined. Some writers have understood en blaith as a veritable "bird of valour," whilst others deem the words as a title for a particular kind of frenzy. I have not met with any statement identifying the bird of valour with the scare-crow, or, indeed, with any bird in particular, although the principal heroes in the Irish battle pieces, from Cuchullain to Murchadh, son of Brian, have each his "Bird of valour" flying over him in the thick of the fight. In the account of the battle of Magh-Rath, we are told that Congal Claen, excited to fury and madness by the exhortations of one of his servants, in the banqueting hall at Dun-na-ngedh, "stood up, assumed his bravery, his heroic fury rose, and his 'bird of valour' fluttered over him, and he distinguished not friend from foe at the time [8]". So when Murchadh, son of Brian after the repulse of the Dal-Cais by the Danes, at the battle of Clontarf, prepares to assail the enemy, it is said that" he was seized with a boiling terrible anger, an excessive elevation and greatness of spirit and mind, A bird of valour and championship rose in him, and fluttered over his head and on his breath.." But this lon laith, en gaile, or bird of valour (?) which hovered about Cuchullain, not oly excited hism ind to fury, as is represented, but also produced a sttrange bodily transformation, from which he obtained the sobriquet of the Riastartha, or transformed. Thus, in a passage in the tale form which I have so often quoted already, where King Ailill deems it advisable to beg Cuychullain's permission for the Connacht army to retire from a position of danger, the following account of the effects of this paroxysm of fury is given:

"Denaid comarli for Ailill, Gudid Conculainn im for lecud asind inudsa ar ni ragaid ar ecin tairis uair rodlebaing a long laith, ar ba ges dosom intan no linged a lon laith ind imreditis a traigthi iarma ocus a escada remi, odus muil a orcan for a lurgnib, ocus in dala suil inachend, ocus araili fria chend anechtair; do coised fer chend for a beolu. Nach findae bid fair ba hathithir delca sciach, ocus banna fola for cach finnu. Ni aithgnead coemu na cairdiu. Cumma no slaided riam ocus iarma. Is desin dober fir nolnecmacht in riastarthu do animm do Coinculainn. (Lebor na hUidhre, fol. 34, b1.)

"'Take counsel together,' said Ailil; 'entreat Cuchullain that he may permit you to leave this place, since you cannot pass by him forcibly, because his lon laith has sprung,'—For it was usually the case with him when his lon laith started in him, that his feet turned backwards and his arms forward, and the calves of his legs were transferred to his shins, and one of his eyes sank deep into his head, whilst the other was protruded, and a man's head would fit in his mouth. Every hair on his head was sharper than then thorns of whitethorn, and a drop of blood stood on each hair. He would not know friends or relations, and he slew equally backwards and forwards. Hence it was that the men of Connacht applied the name of 'Riastartha' to Cuchullainn."

It has been already observed that the name of the goddess, o fury, whose identity we have been endeavouring to connect with Cathu-bodua, is written badb and bodb, just as the adjectives derived therefrom are written badba and bodba, and the driv. subst. badbdacht and bodbdacht.

The term bodba (terrible) is applied to the Morrigan in an old tract in the book of Leinster, where Conor Mac Nessa is represented as directing Findchad to summon auxiliaries to assist Cuchullainn: "ardotrai cosin nathaig mbodba, cosin Mórriagain co dún Sobairche;" "go to the terrible fury, to the Morrigan, to Dun-Sobairche (Dunseverick, co.Antrim)."

The name Morrigan is also varied, as we have seen, to Morrigu; but as the genitive form is Morrigna, the proper nom. would seem to be Morrigan.

In the Irish mythological tracts a well-marked distinction is observable between the attributes of the scald-crow and those of the raven; the scald-crow, or cornix, being represented in the written as in the spoken traditions of the country, not alone as a bird of ill omen, but as an agen in the fulfilment of what is "in dono" in dan, or decreed for a person, whilst the raven is simply regarded as a bird of prey, that follows the warrior merely for the sake of enjoying its gory feast. Juast as the German myths describe Odin and Zio as accompanied by ravens and wolves, which folow them to the battle field, and prey upon the slain, so the Irish poets, in their laugations of particular heroes, boast of the number of ravens and wolves fed by their spears. Odin, especially, had two ravens, wise and cunning, which sa upon his shoulders and whispered into his ears, like Mahomet's pigeon, all that they had heard and seen [9].In this latter respect the raven of German mythology stands in the same relation to Odin thta the raven of Greek mythology does to Apollo. The scandinavians, like their German relatives, considered the raven in a sacred light.

The Anglo-Saxon chronicle (at the year 878) records the capture from the Norse of a banner called the Raven, of which a more particular account is in Asser's Life of Alfred, at the same year. After describing the defeat of the Pagan Norse before Kynwith castle. On Devonshire, the writer adds, "and there they (the West Saxons) gained very large booty, and amongst other thngs the banner called the Raven; for they say that the three sisters of Hingwar and Hubba, daughters of Lodbrok, wove tht flag and got it ready in one day, They say, moreover that in every battle, wherever that flag went before them, if they were to gain the victory, a live crow would appear flying on the middle of the flag; but if they were doomed to be defeated it would hang down motionles; and this was often proved to be so." Earl Sigurd also is said to have had a raen banner at the battle of Clontarf, which his mother had woven for him with magical skill [10].

This idea fo the raven banner is probably connected with the tradition given in the Vœlsûnga-Saga, which represents Odin as sending the Valkyria Oskemey, in the form of a crow, on a mission to Friga, to entreat that the wife of King Reris might become fruitful [11]; and the prayer being heard, a son (Sigmund) was born, whose son Sigurd married Brunhilt, a Valkyria, who was kalled Kraka, or the crow, and who was the wife of Radnar Lodbrok, and mother of Ivar Beinlaus.

The Morrigan has some dim connetion to the pagan festival of Samhain, or Allhallowtide. Macha Mongruadh, the fabled foundress of Ard-Macha (Armagh) whose sword (chaidhem Macha Moingruadh) is described as a very powerful weapon, is sometimes Morrigan; as is also Mongfind, a great queen of the 3rd cent., in whose honour the festival of Samhain was anciently called "Feil-Moing," "when the vulger and women asked requests of her." (Book of Ballymote.)

The name of the Morrigan is found connected with many of the fulachts, or Kitchen Middens, particularly with the larger ones, which are called "Fulacht na Morrigna," the "Morrigan's hearth," whilst the smaller ones are named "Fulacht Fian. One of these great Fulachts at Tara would cook three kinds of food at the same time. Some account of it wil be found in Petrie's "Antiquities of Tara," pp. 213-14 (where, however, Petrie should have considered it rather a cauldron than a spit). In the tract call the dthe Agallamh beg, or "Little Dialogue," contained in the "Book of Lismore" mention is made (fol. 196 a2) of another

Fulacht-na-Morrigna which existed near the fairy mound of Sidh-Airfemhin, in the present countyof Tipperary.

"Ba hiat fein do rinde both doibh ind oidchi sin, ocus do rinded indeonadh leo, ocuss teit Cailte ocus Findchadh do indlad a lámha cum int srotha. Inad fulachta so ar Findchad, ocus is cian o do rinded. Is fir ar Cailte, ocus fulacht na Morrighna so, ocus ni denta gan uisce." "It was they who made a hut for themselves that night; and indeonad (cooking places wer made by them And Cailte and Findchadh went to the stream to wash their hands. 'Here is the site of a fulacht, 'said Finchadh and it is a long time since it was made.' 'True,' said Cailte; 'and this is a fulacht-na-Morrighna which is not to be made without water'" (i. e.there should be a supply of water near at hand).

The name of the Morrigan enters not a little into the composition of Irish topographical names. In the present county of Louth there is a district anciently known by the name of Gort-na-Morrigna, of the "Morrigan's feild,"which her husband, the Dagda, had given to her("Book of Fermoy," fol. 125, a2). The "Book of Lismore" (fol. 196, b1) mentions a Crich-na-Morrigna, as somewhere in the present county of Wicklow. Among the remarkable monuments of the Brugh on the Boyne were Mur=na-Morrigna (the mound of the Morrigan); two hills called the Cirr and Cuirrel (or comb and brush) of the Dagda's wife, which Dr. Petrie has inadvertently transformed into two proper names; and Da cich na Morrigna, or the "Morrigan's two paps." The name of the Morrigan is also probably contained in that of Tirreeworrigan, in the county of Armagh.

W. M. Hennessy.

P. S.—Mr. Hennessy's preceding paper is a valuable contribution to the comparative mythology of the Germans (chiefly Scandinavians) and Celts. More than one element of the

Badhbh-story is common to both races. I mention briefly the chief coincindences.

I. To the ancient Irish goddesses of war correspond to the Norwegian (and, in general, Germanic) Valkyrias.

II. These Irish goddesses appear either by themselves, or (when more than one) three in number. In a similar way the Norns appear three together, and the youngest of them, Skuld, is at the same time a Valkyria. Very often too, three Valkyrias fly together (Vœlundarquidha, 1, 2).

III. One of these goddesses is often the special companion of one hero, assists and warns him and, when his hour has come, leaves him with a cry. Instances of love-stories of a supernatural character are numerous in Germanic mythology. « Sigurd and Brynhild » furnish one. But the finest of the stories in the Older Edda, in the songsof Helgi. I do not find however that in Germanic tales the approaching death is announceed by the divine bride leaving her husband with sorrow. Perhaps there may have been something of that kind in Sigurd's murder committed at the instigation of Brynhild. The dying Helgi too says to his Valkyrian bride: « Do you not sorrow, you have been destruction. » Herein seems to lurk a conception more stern than the Irish, namelythat the Valkyrian herself is, when time arrives, the instrument of her lover's death. The simply divine Valkyrias that live with Odhinn and are not attached to any particular man, are sent by him for the special purpose of calling the heroes « home ». Hence in fact the name VAlkyria, « the chooser of the slain » (Norse val-r, strages; kiosa, eligere).

IV. The Irish goddesses appear in the form of a bird, which is more especially considered as the « bird of valour » of the hero. It is not always easy to find out what exact form they assume, but it is genearally that of a scaldcrow. The Germanic Valkyrias generally appear as swans. Yet the Vœlsunga Saga tells of love between one of Sigurd's ancestors and a Valkyria, who assumed the figure of a crow, and Aslaug, daughter of Sigurd, who accompanies Ragnar Lodbrok after the fashion of the Valkyrias, calls herself also « crow » (kraka).

V. The names of the Irish goddesses, as far as can be ascertained, are Badb, (or Badb-catha) Fea, Ana, Morrigu (or Morrigan) Macha, Neman. Perhaps we might be justified in comparing the name of Macha with gr. μάχη. As far as the first of these names is concerned it is certainly identical witn M. Pictet's [C]athubodua and it has its conter-part in Germany. Tacitus tells us (Ann. IV, 73) that, in the eventful campaign of the Romans against the Frisians, nine hundred Romans were slain « apud lucum quem Baduhennæ vocant. » This must be understood « Near the wood which is consecrated to Baduhennæ. » Now Badu is a Germanic word for « strife » (Anglo-Saxon beado, Old-Norse boedhr). Indeed it does not appear as the name of a Valkyria; but when oen thinks that by the side of nemas in—hild decidedly derived from the Valkyrias such as Mahthild, Gundhild, Svanhild, there appears an Old-High German woman-name Baduhild which indirectly confirms the statement of Tacitus, it becomes most probably that there was an ancient Germanic goddess of war, named Badu.

Such similarieites between German and Celtic traditions cannot be accidental. Not even the historical connection of the Scandinavians and the Irish can explain them. It seems that we must go much further back, to those times when along the Rhine Celts and Germans mixed together, sometimes as friends, sometimes as foes, when the king of the Marcomans, Maroboduus, a German by birth, assumed a Celtic name, in the same way as in later times Cormac, Nial, went over to the Scandinavians from Celtic lips. The old Gaulish names Caturix, Toutiorix,

Segomaros, Albiorix, have their Germanic corresponding words (some of which are still in use) in the names Hedrich, Dietrich, Sigmar, Alberich.

All these instances of resemblance indicate a long intercourse, and songs and traditions, as well as names and words, may have been interchanged from one side of the Rhine to the other and have strenghtened the old bonds which united Celts and Germans in the time of the Indogermanic unity.

C. Lottner.

ENDNOTES

[1] Nous devons à la bienveillance de la Revue Archéologique de pouvoir reproduire ici la representation du monument original qui accompagnait l'article de M. Pictet. Cette copie est une reduction au dixième, obtenue par la pantographe sur un estampage – H.G. (p. 1)

[2] See the Dream of Rhonabwy, in the Mabinogion, part. V, pp. 385 and 410. (p. 3)

[3] It is rather an interesting fact that near the mountain called Da-Cich-Anann, there is a fort called Lis-Babha, or the fort of the Badb. (p. 8)

[4] Book of Leinster, fol.5, b2. (p. 8)

[5] Book of Leinster, fol. 189, b1. (p. 9)

[6] See also the reference to badbs and furies in the Battle of Magh-Lena, pp. 130-1, sq. (p. 10)

[7] Ms. Trin. Coll. Dublin H. 2, 17, fol. 97, a. (p. 10)

[8] Battle of Magh-Rath, p. 33. (p. 28)

[9] Grimm, Deutsche Mythologie2, p. 134. (p. 30)

[10] Todd's "Danish wars," introd. p. clxxxiij, note 1. (p. 31)

[11] Fornaldar Sœgur, Copenagen, 1825, pp. 117-118. (p. 31)

www.ingramcontent.com/pod-product-compliance
Lightning Source LLC
Chambersburg PA
CBHW051554010526
44118CB00022B/2705